Mac Can Do It!

by Dale Cooper

illustrated by Linda Howard Bittner

Scott Foresman
is an imprint of

Glenview, Illinois • Boston, Massachusetts • Chandler, Arizona
Upper Saddle River, New Jersey

Every effort has been made to secure permission and provide appropriate credit for photographic material. The publisher deeply regrets any omission and pledges to correct errors called to its attention in subsequent editions.

Unless otherwise acknowledged, all photographs are the property of Scott Foresman, a division of Pearson Education.

Photo locators denoted as follows: Top (T), Center (C), Bottom (B), Left (L), Right (R), Background (Bkgd)

Illustrations by Linda Howard Bittner

Photograph 12 Digital Vision

ISBN 13: 978-0-328-50751-1
ISBN 10:   0-328-50751-2

11 12 13 14 15 V010 17 16 15 14 13

Once there was a family.
They had a baby boy.
Mac was not just any boy.
At one week old, he could talk.

Mac was not just any boy.
At two weeks old, he could run!
"There is a race outside," said Dad.
"I will run past everyone," said Mac.

"Are you sure you are old enough?"
said Dad.

"Yes, I can do it on my own,"
said Mac.

And Mac won the race!

Mac was not just any boy.
At three weeks old, he could fix things!
"Will we ever fix this sink?" said Mom.
"I will fix it!" said Mac.

"Are you sure you are old enough?"
said Mom.

"Yes, I can do it on my own,"
said Mac.

And Mac fixed the sink!

Mac was not just any boy.
At four weeks old, he could
read numbers!
   "Our mailman is sick today," said Dad.
   "I will do his job," said Mac.

"Are you sure you are old enough?" said Dad.

"Yes, I can read the mailbox numbers on my own," said Mac.

And Mac gave out the mail!

Mac was not just any boy.
At five weeks old, he flew a spaceship!
Mom and Dad were watching.
"Will you go to the moon?" they said.

Mac is born.	One week old:	Two weeks old:
	Mac talks.	Mac wins a race.

"Yes, I can fly there on my own,"
said Mac.
      And he did.

Three weeks old:	Four weeks old:	Five weeks old:
Mac fixes the sink.	Mac gives out the mail.	Mac flies a spaceship.

Different Ways To Grow

A human baby does not walk until the baby is around one year old. But many animals walk sooner than that. A baby elephant learns to stand as soon as it is born. A baby reindeer must run to keep up with the herd. It runs soon after birth.

Most baby birds spend their first few weeks in the nest. Then they learn to fly so that they can find food. As soon as baby dolphins are born, they swim to the surface. They need to take their first breath.

Every living thing grows differently.